THIS IS THE
BEAR

RE-PLAYED BY
VIVIAN FRENCH

FROM THE BOOK BY
SARAH HAYES AND HELEN CRAIG

WALKER BOOKS
AND SUBSIDIARIES
LONDON • BOSTON • SYDNEY

D1322989

First published 2000 by Walker Books Ltd
87 Vauxhall Walk, London SE11 5HJ

2 4 6 8 10 9 7 5 3 1

Playscript © 2000 Vivian French
Original text © 1986 Sarah Hayes
Illustrations © 1986 Helen Craig

This book has been typeset in Goudy.

Printed in Singapore

British Library Cataloguing in Publication Data
A catalogue record for this book is
available from the British Library.

ISBN 0-7445-7266-5

Notes for Children

This Is the Bear is the story of
a bear who is lost and a boy who looks for him.
You may know the story already, but it doesn't
matter if you don't.

This book is a little different from other picture books.
You will be sharing it with other people and telling
the story together.

You can read

this line

this line

this line

or this line.

Even when someone else is reading, try to follow the words.
It will help when it's your turn!

I can see a bear!

What's he saying?

What's going on?

Read us the story!

This is the bear

Who fell in the bin.

This is the dog

Who pushed him in.

The bear's in the bin!

What's the bear saying?

He says, "Oh no!"

Poor bear!

I can see a man.

I can see a bag.

Where's the bear?

The bear's in the bag!

This is the man

Who picked up the sack.

This is the driver

Who would not come back.

The bear's in the bag.

The bag's in the lorry.

The lorry's driving away!

It's driving away with the bear!

Look!

There's the bear!

He's falling out of the bag.

He's falling in the rubbish.

This is the bear

Who went to the dump

And fell on the pile

With a bit of a bump.

Poor bear!

There's a lot of rubbish.

I can see a mouse!

Eek! There's a mouse!

Ouch!

There's a big blue bus.

The boy's stopping the bus.

Stop! Stop!

Stop the bus!

This is the boy

Who took the bus

And went to the dump

To make a fuss.

I can't see the bear.

The boy looks cross.

The boy *is* cross!

He wants his bear.

What's the boy doing?

He's looking in the bag.

He's looking for his bear.

This is the man

In an awful grump

Who searched

And searched

And searched the dump.

Will they find the bear?

I can't see him.

The boy's very sad.

The dog's feeling bad.

There's the bear!

Can they see him?

Will they find him?

Look at all that rubbish!

This is the bear

All cold and cross

Who did not think

He was really lost.

The bear can see the boy.

The boy's still sad.

Look at the man!

Look where he's looking!

Here I am.

What's the dog doing?

He's sniffing!

Can he smell the bear?

Read us the story!

This is the dog

Who smelled the smell

Of a bone.

What about the bear?

Dogs like bones.

Oh.

What is it?

I want to see the bear!

The dog's sniffing again.

What's he sniffing?

This is the dog

Who smelled the smell

Of a bone

And a tin

And a bear as well.

He's found the bear!

What was in the tin?

I don't know.

Where's the bone?

I don't know!

Hello, Fred.

What's happening now?

I can see the dog.

What's going on?

Tell us the story!

This is the man

Who drove them home.

The boy, the bear

And the dog with a bone.

The dog's got the bone.

The boy's got his bear.

The boy's happy.

Hurrah!

The bear's in the bath.

Scrub-a-dub-dub.

There's a bear in a tub!

Scrub-a-dub-dub!

This is the bear

All lovely and clean

Who did not say

Just where he had been.

The bear's not telling.

I know where he's been!

So do I.

So do I.

A little trip.

What's the boy wearing?

He's wearing his pyjamas.

Is he going to bed?

Wait and see!

This is the boy

Who knew quite well,

But promised his friend

He would not tell.

Shh!

Shh!

It's a secret.

Don't tell!

I will.

And this is the boy

Who woke up in the night

And asked the bear

If he felt all right –

And was very surprised

When the bear shouted out,

"How soon can we have

Another day out?"

Notes for Teachers

Story Plays are written and presented in a way that encourages children to read aloud together. They are dramatic versions of memorable and exciting stories, told in strongly patterned language which gives children the chance to practise at a vital stage of their reading development. Sharing stories in this way makes reading an active and enjoyable process, and one that draws in even the reticent reader.

The story is told by four different voices, divided into four colours so that each child can easily read his or her part. The blue line is for more experienced readers; the red line for less experienced readers. When there are more than four children in a group, there is an ideal opportunity for paired reading. Partnering a more experienced reader with a less experienced one can be very supportive and provides a learning experience for both children.

Story Plays encourage children to share in the reading of a whole text in a collaborative and interactive way. This makes them perfect for group and guided reading activities. Children will find they need to pay close attention to the print and punctuation, and to use the meaning of the whole story in order to read it with expression and a real sense of voice.

The Big Book version can be used to introduce children to *Story Plays* in shared reading sessions. The class can be divided into groups to take part in reading the text aloud together, creating a lively performance.